I0408327

Advance Policy Questions for the Honorable Brad R. Carson, Nominee for Under Secretary of Defense for Personnel and Readiness

Defense Reforms

The Committee has recently held a series of hearings on defense reform.

What modifications of Goldwater-Nichols Department of Defense Reorganization Act of 1986 provisions, if any, do you believe would be appropriate?

The Department of Defense is currently undergoing a similar review that has been informed by the hearings the Committee has held. The ongoing review is quite broad with respect to its scope and includes topics such as the appropriate role of the Joint Staff, the joint acquisitions process, and the appropriate command and control structure for our cyber workforce. I would not presume to offer opinions on topics beyond the scope of the position for which I've been nominated; however, several topics directly impact my prospective portfolio as the Under Secretary of Defense for Personnel and Readiness. My own personal opinion is that a re-evaluation of the definition of "Joint Matters" is required; the current definition must be expanded to recognize the increasing exposure to joint operations that officers face, particularly at a younger age, and better reflect the unique role our reserve components play in disaster relief and homeland defense. Additionally, I believe there is a fundamental tension between career timelines associated with the Defense Officer Personal Management Act (DOPMA) and the requirements for promotion to General/Flag officer under the Goldwater-Nichols Act; this tension is particularly acute, ironically, for our highest performing officers. I would be in favor of re-evaluating the current 36 month statutory requirement for accredited joint tours and moving to a more experiential-based system. Finally, I believe a comprehensive paradigm shift is required for joint qualification. The Military Services currently operate under a one-size-fits-all model that is inadequate to the current operating environment. I would be in favor of moving to something closer to a "joint continuum" that includes options for both breadth and depth in joint matters, depending on the officer's particular skill set. This system could, perhaps, tier the requirements for joint experience and education to better reflect current needs in the joint community and within the Military Services.

Qualifications

What background and experience do you have that you believe qualifies you for this position?

I believe that, if confirmed, my diverse political, military, legal, and business experiences have well prepared me to execute the duties of the Under Secretary of Defense for Personnel and Readiness. I previously had the honor and privilege of serving as the General Counsel of the Army, a position in which I have had legal oversight of every issue arising from the Army's global operations. In addition to myriad routine matters, I assisted Secretary of the

Army John McHugh in developing military-wide responses to particularly vexing problems and issues, such as ensuring that Soldiers with behavioral health conditions are properly diagnosed, creating wholesome environments at all Army child development centers, and eradicating sexual assault. More generally, I have been asked to provide advice at nearly every meeting of the Army's senior leaders, where issues of readiness, modernization, operations, and personnel are discussed and decided. More recently, I was Under Secretary of the Army. In that role, I was the chief management officer of the Service. I led, among other things, the delayering of Army headquarters and a wholescale revision to The Army Plan.

It is helpful to also briefly summarize my education and professional career. Before joining the Department of the Army, I was a professor in the College of Business and the College of Law at the University of Tulsa, where I led a research institute devoted to energy issues and taught courses in property law, energy policy, negotiations and game theory, and globalization. I attended Baylor University, where I graduated with highest honors and was inducted into Phi Beta Kappa. Studying as a Rhodes Scholar at Trinity College, Oxford, I earned a B.A./M.A. in Politics, Philosophy, and Economics. Upon returning to the United States, I graduated from the University of Oklahoma College Of Law, where I was recognized as the Outstanding Graduate. I entered the practice of law at Crowe & Dunlevy, the largest firm in the state of Oklahoma. During my early years of legal work, I focused on commercial litigation, with a particular emphasis on antitrust. From 1997 through 1998, I was a White House Fellow, serving in the Department of Defense. After completing the White House Fellowship, I returned to practicing commercial litigation at Crowe & Dunlevy. In 2000, I was elected to represent the 2nd District of Oklahoma in the United States House of Representatives. As a Congressman, I worked closely with other members of the Oklahoma delegation to protect and enhance the state's military installations. In 2005, after leaving politics, I was a fellow at the Kennedy School of Government at Harvard University. Thereafter, I was a Director and then Chief Executive Officer of CNB, LLC. From 2008 to 2009, as an officer in the United States Navy, I served in Iraq on active military duty with the 84th Explosive Ordnance Battalion of the United States Army, as the Officer-in-Charge of Weapons Intelligence Teams in Multi-National Division-South. For my service, I was awarded the Bronze Star and Army Achievement Medal.

I believe that these varied experiences have prepared me for the extraordinary challenge of serving as Under Secretary of Defense for Personnel and Readiness. If confirmed, I will commit to using my skills and experience to diligently and effectively perform the duties of Under Secretary.

Major Challenges

In your view, what are the major challenges confronting the next Under Secretary of Defense for Personnel and Readiness?

The Under Secretary of Defense for Personnel and Readiness oversees one of the broadest portfolios in the Department of Defense. The next Under Secretary will have to confront complex questions about the appropriate workforce mix (among civilians, contractors, and military personnel) in an era of declining budgets; work with the Joint

Staff and Under Secretary of Defense for Policy to investigate and implement new models for strategic readiness and tactical readiness reporting to improve the options we offer to the President and National Command Authority; examine questions of appropriate force mix between active and reserve components as the Military Services undergo endstrength reductions; and seek to better balance the fundamental tensions in the Military Health System, which seeks to provide the best possible health care to our beneficiaries and simultaneously produce a ready medical force.

If confirmed, what plans do you have for addressing these challenges?

If confirmed, I hope to work with the Congress, this Committee, and my colleagues within the Department of Defense to develop the best possible strategies and policies that will address these critical issues.

Duties

Section 136 of Title 10, United States Code, provides that the Under Secretary of Defense for Personnel and Readiness shall perform such duties and exercise such powers as the Secretary of Defense may prescribe in the areas of military readiness, total force management, military and civilian personnel requirements, military and civilian personnel training, military and civilian family matters, exchange, commissary, and non-appropriated fund activities, personnel requirements for weapons support, National Guard and reserve components, and health affairs..

Assuming you are confirmed, what duties do you expect to be assigned to you?

The duties I expect to carry out are my responsibilities, functions, relationships, and authorities, in accordance with the law and consistent with DoD Directive 5124.2, "Under Secretary of Defense for Personnel and Readiness (USD (P&R))." I will serve the Secretary of Defense as his principal staff assistant and advisor in all matters relating to the management and well-being of the DoD Total Force and the oversight of the readiness of this Force, particularly as it relates to manpower; force management; planning; program integration; readiness; National Guard and Reserve component affairs; health affairs; training; personnel requirements and management; and compensation. I also expect to carry out the Secretary's priority in ensuring that the Department can recruit and retain a force of the future with the right capabilities for future warfighting.

In carrying out these duties, what would be your relationship with the following officials?

- **The Secretary of Defense**

  If confirmed, I will serve the Secretary of Defense as his principal advisor and advocate for Total Force Management and Readiness; military and civilian personnel policy; military health care and medical readiness; training; and personnel requirements and management, including equal opportunity, morale, welfare, recreation, and quality of life matters.

- **The Deputy Secretary of Defense**

  If confirmed, I would expect my relationship with the Deputy Secretary to be functionally the same as that with the Secretary of Defense.

- **The Assistant Secretary of Defense for Manpower and Reserve Affairs**

  If confirmed, ASD (M&RA) will be my principal advisor for all force management, Reserve affairs, family support, and personnel policies.

- **The Assistant Secretary of Defense for Health Affairs**

  If confirmed, ASD (HA) will be my principal advisor for all DoD health policies, programs, and force health protection activities.

- **The Department of Defense General Counsel**

  If confirmed, I expect that I will seek and follow the advice of the General Counsel on legal and procedural matters pertaining to the policies promulgated from the off ices of the USD (P&R), and in so doing, have regular communication, coordination of actions, and exchange of views with the General Counsel and the attorneys assigned to focus on personnel policy matters.

- **The Department of Defense Inspector General**

  If confirmed, I will fully assist the DoD Inspector General—in charge of promoting integrity, accountability, and improvement of Department of Defense personnel, programs—in any investigations or issues that relate to personnel and readiness.

- **The Service Secretaries**

  If confirmed, I anticipate working closely with the Secretaries of the Military Departments on all matters relating to the management, well-being, and readiness of military and civilian personnel in the DoD Total Force structure.

- **The Service Chiefs**

  If confirmed, I also anticipate working closely with the Secretaries of the Military Departments on all matters relating to the Total Force management, well-being, and readiness of military and civilian personnel throughout the Department.

- **The Chief of the National Guard Bureau**

  If confirmed, I plan to work closely with the Chief, National Guard Bureau to ensure effective integration of National Guard capabilities into a cohesive Total Force.

- **The Assistant Secretaries for Manpower and Reserve Affairs of the Army, Navy, and Air Force**

  If confirmed, I look forward to working closely with these officials in carrying out the human resource obligations of the Services for the Total Force.

- **The Deputy Chiefs of Staff of the Army and Air Force for Personnel, the Chief of Naval Personnel, and the Deputy Commandant of the Marine Corps for Manpower and Reserve Affairs**

  If confirmed, I look forward to effective working relationships with these officers to ensure that DoD attracts, motivates and retains the quality people it needs.

- **The Chiefs of the Army, Navy, and Air Force Reserves and the Commander of the U.S. Marine Corps Forces Reserve**

  If confirmed, I will build strong relationship to ensure effective integration of Reserve Component capabilities into a cohesive Total Force.

- **The combatant commanders**

  If confirmed, I intend work closely with the Combatant Commanders on all matters relating to the management, well-being, and readiness of the DoD Total Force.

- **The Joint Staff, particularly the Director for Manpower and Personnel (J-1)**

  If confirmed, I would hope to establish a closely coordinated relationship with the Joint Staff regarding manpower and personnel policy issues.

- **The Director, Defense Health Agency**

  If confirmed, I will enlist the advice of the Director of the Defense Health Agency, through ASD (HA), in all matter relating to the Military Health System and common medical services shared across all Services.

- **The Director, Office of Personnel Management**

If confirmed, I hope to cultivate a close working relationship with the Director, Office of Personnel Management on matters regarding civilian personnel policies.

Prevention of and Response to Sexual Assaults

What is your assessment of the current DOD sexual assault prevention and response program?

We aspire to eliminate sexual assault, and we still have work to do. Even so, empirical evidence suggests the program, which is a constant work-in-progress, is making things better. Sexual assault prevalence as measured by the most recent surveys indicates that the estimated occurrence of sexual assault is at its lowest level since surveys began for active duty Service members in 2010. At the same time, reporting of these incidents is at an all-time high. We also know that victims have positively reviewed many of the reforms introduced, including the Special Victims Counsel program.

What is your view of the provision for restricted and unrestricted reporting of sexual assaults?

Our goals are to decrease sexual assaults, to ensure that victims receive comprehensive care, and to hold offenders appropriately accountable. More than 5000 victims have opted to use restricted reporting since 2005. Without such an option to file a restricted report, these victims might not have received the care they needed. I am pleased that the percentage of Service members choosing to convert their restricted report to an unrestricted report and participate in an investigation has been increasing, from approximately 15% to about 20% in the recent year. These report conversions are an indicator of growing confidence in the DoD response.

What is your view of the adequacy of DOD oversight of military service implementation of the DOD and service policies for the prevention of and response to sexual assaults?

The Department has a number of oversight mechanisms, including monthly meetings, chaired by the SAPRO Director, with the Service sexual assault program chiefs. These meetings review Service progress with regard to execution of the DoD-wide Strategic Plan, Secretary of Defense initiatives, and related provisions of the National Defense Authorization Act.

The Department also uses the Annual Report to Congress, in which the Secretary of Defense assesses the Services' input, as an oversight opportunity.

Additionally, we hear regularly from survivors, and this feedback permits us to assess the kind of support being provided them, as well as to identify and address any gaps in our response system.

What is your view about the role of the chain of command in changing the military culture in which these sexual assaults have occurred?

Commanders and leaders at all levels are central to the Department's approach to foster a command climate where sexist behaviors, sexual harassment, and sexual assault are not condoned or ignored – and where reporters of all misconduct receive the support they need. We select and train our commanders and leaders to uphold high ethical and moral standards themselves and in the troops they lead, and much of the recent progress comes from our ability to use the chain of command as agents of change. The Department has provided commanders with a number of tools to prevent and respond to this crime, including pre-command training, a unit climate assessment process, and a sexual assault case management system in place at each installation. DoD surveys indicate that survivors are satisfied with the support they've received from unit commanders. That being said, we are always looking for ways help commanders empower their people to intervene appropriately in situations at risk for sexual assault and other harms.

Surveys report that up to 62 percent of victims who report a sexual assault perceive professional or social retaliation for reporting. If confirmed, what will you do to address the issue of retaliation for reporting a sexual assault?

All victims of crime, including those who experience sexual assault, should feel free to report without fear of reprisal, ostracism, or some other form of maltreatment. It is unacceptable that so many sexual assault victims perceive a price associated with coming forward to the Department. Our new *Retaliation Prevention and Response Strategy* increases oversight and accountability; aligns prevention and response efforts across the Services; improves data collection and analysis to understand the scope of the problem; and further empowers response personnel to escalate cases of retaliation. We are currently working to implement this strategy across the Department.

Sexual assault is a significantly underreported crime in our society and in the military. If confirmed, what will you do to increase reporting of sexual assaults by military victims?

In the ten years that the Sexual Assault Prevention and Response Program has been in place, reports have increased by 260%, from 1,700 to 6,131 per year. Even while we work to drive the number of assaults down, we continue efforts to increase the proportion of victims who report. We are also taking steps to encourage male victims, who studies suggest are less inclined to report a sexual assault, to come forward and report incidents of sexual assaults and receive appropriate care.

In your view, what would be the impact of requiring a judge advocate outside the chain of command, instead of a military commander in the grade of O-6 or above as is currently the Department's policy, to determine whether allegations of sexual assault should be prosecuted?

I understand that the Response Systems Panel, an independent, Congressionally-mandated panel looked at a similar question on the impact of removing convening authority from commanders. A majority of the panel members (7-2) concluded that the evidence they reviewed did not support the conclusion that removing convening authority from commanders would reduce the incidence of sexual assaults, or increase reporting by victims, or improve the quality of investigations and prosecutions of sexual assault.

Recently, the Department has implemented a series of changes to help the Department address allegations of sexual assault and hold offenders appropriately accountable, and we are still assessing their impact on the military justice. Moreover, the Military Justice Review Group published a set of reform recommendations aimed at modernizing and increasing justice and efficiency within the UCMJ. It is my understanding that the Department is currently focused on this comprehensive set of reforms aimed at improving prosecution and defense of all crimes.

If confirmed, I will continue to collaborate with the DoD General Counsel, the DoD Inspector General, and the military legal communities on what can be done to improve the investigation and adjudication of sexual assault allegations. We will also continue to work with the Judicial Proceedings Panel and the soon to be created Defense Advisory Committee on Investigation, Prosecution, and Defense of Sexual Assault in the Armed Forces as they make recommendations on these matters.

Sexual Harassment

Department of Defense annual sexual assault reports document that the sexual assaults are more common in units where sexual harassment is prevalent. Section 579 of the National Defense Authorization Act (NDAA) for Fiscal Year 2013 required the Secretary of Defense to develop a comprehensive policy to prevent and respond to sexual harassment in the Armed Forces and to submit a report to the Committees on Armed Services of the Senate and House of Representatives no later than January 2, 2013, setting forth a the comprehensive policy. The committee still has not yet received this report.

Do you agree with the premise that units with a command climate that tolerates sexual harassment is more likely to have increased incidents of sexual assault?

We know from research that sexual harassment does lead to some types of sexual assault. This is but one of many reasons we should be concerned about unhealthy command climates. To specifically address this, the Department adjusted our surveys to provide commanders with better tools for assessing command climate. For example, we reframed survey questions to more pointedly focus on indications of sexual harassment. Surveys also measure perceived leadership support, and organizational knowledge of reporting options, which informs key elements of prevention and intervention training. These enhanced instruments provide leaders at all levels with better insight into how to prevent and respond to these behaviors.

What is the reason the Department has not complied with the requirement to develop a comprehensive sexual harassment policy?

The Department has struggled to develop a sufficiently comprehensive and effective sexual harassment policy. We are currently engaged with the Services to articulate the objectives of the policy and map those objectives to concrete, actionable policy items. The new Force Resiliency Directorate has engaged with your staffs to ensure Congressional perspectives are reflected in the policy. I will ensure this effort continues expediently and that my staff remains engaged with yours.

If confirmed, will you assure this committee that the Department will promptly promulgate a comprehensive policy to prevent and respond to sexual harassment in the Armed Forces and to submit this policy to the Committees on Armed Services of the Senate and House of Representatives as directed in the Fiscal Year 2013 NDAA?

Yes, the Department will continue to codify existing guidance into an updated and comprehensive DoD instruction. We are currently engaged with the Services to articulate the objectives of the policy and map those objectives to concrete, actionable policy items. The new Force Resiliency Directorate has engaged with your staffs to ensure Congressional perspectives are reflected in the policy. I will ensure this effort continues expediently and that my staff remains engaged with yours.

Hazing

In a report released on February 9, 2016, the Government Accountability Office released a report that the Department of Defense has limited visibility over hazing incidents involving service members and does not know the extent to which hazing policies issued by DOD and the military services have been implemented.

If confirmed, what actions will you take to monitor implementation of DOD and military service hazing policies?

We recently issued a new Total Force Hazing and Bullying Prevention and Response policy memorandum to reinforce our position on this important topic. The memorandum provided updated definitions of hazing and bullying and examples of activities likely to be considered to be problematic. Our guidance provides better clarity on what is or is not hazing and mandates standardized incident tracking and reporting which will inform preventive training and education.

In addition, the Department is also currently working to codify elements of the policy memorandum into a new DoD instruction to further clarify roles and responsibilities, incident reporting and investigation, victim/complainant assistance procedures, and training requirements.

If confirmed, will you issue guidance on the collection and tracking of hazing incident data?

I will monitor the Services' hazing prevention and response policies for effectiveness and to identify best practices across the Department and will ensure that individual Services adjust their programs as necessary to increase their effectiveness. As part of this effort, the Office of Diversity Management and Equal Opportunity meets regularly with the Services to review policy implementation, reporting procedures, and on-going complainant assistance. These interactions permit us to identify systemic issues and provide additional guidance on tracking, prevention, and training as necessary.

How will you and the Department of Defense evaluate the prevalence of hazing in the military?

We will continue to work directly with the Services as they review and analyze newly-standardized data from reported incidents. We will also continue to derive insights from the newly-improved command climate and workforce survey instruments that allow us to make targeted adjustments to training, policy, and procedures to ensure all Service members recognize, report, and respond to problematic behaviors. The Defense Equal Opportunity Management Institute Organizational Climate Survey is one such instrument that enables the Department to assess critical organizational climate dimensions at unit level and in aggregate roll-up form.

Service Academies

What do you consider to be the policy and procedural elements that must be in place at each of the service academies in order to prevent and respond appropriately to sexual assaults and sexual harassment and to ensure essential oversight?

Each of the Military Service Academies has robust policies, programs, and personnel in place to support the Sexual Assault Prevention and Response Program. Academy prevention programs are working to create a long-term approach to changing how people view their role in social settings at risk for sexual assault and sexual harassment. They are empowering all to take meaningful preventive action. Academy response programs are also effective at delivering support and other recovery resources to victims of sexual assault and those who file sexual harassment complaints. The last element that the Academies require is the development of metrics to help academy leadership better guide sexual assault and sexual harassment programs. We addressed this need in our last Military Service Academy report in January, and expect to see a suite of metrics from each in the forthcoming year.

What is your assessment of measures taken at the service academies to ensure religious tolerance and respect, and to prevent sexual assaults and sexual harassment?

Current Department policy places a high value on the rights of members of the Military Services to observe the tenets of their respective religions or to observe no religion at all. The policies at the Service Academies neither encourage nor discourage discussions of religion by individual Service members.

While there is always more work to be done, evidence shows the prevention efforts at the Academies have been effective. Sexual assault prevalence as measured by the most recent surveys indicates that those rates are at lowest levels since surveys began for the Academies in 2005. Each of the Superintendents provides direct program oversight and we have seen significant improvements at all three Academies due to their involvement. Academy leadership attention drives continued progress and leaders continue to address the behaviors and attitudes that predicate these offenses. All the Academies are in compliance with the Department's policies regarding sexual harassment and sexual assault. In addition, all three Academies also go far beyond what is required in policy for their prevention and response programs. Our most recent Military Service Academy Report in January provided substantive evidence of these efforts.

Assignment Policies for Women in the Military

On December 3, 2015 Secretary of Defense Carter announced that the Department will open all military combat positions to women.

In your view, will this decision strengthen the armed forces? If so, how?

Yes. The Department will now have access to additional individuals who can add strength to the joint force and assign the most qualified individual to occupations and positions.

Do you believe that the services' implementation plans should be based on bona fide military requirements? If so, what steps would you take to ensure that such decisions are made on this basis?

Yes. The Department of Defense is a standards-based organization and will continue to be one. I personally reviewed each of the implementation plans and participate in the Implementation Work Group co-chaired by the Deputy Secretary of Defense and the Vice Chairman of the Joint Chiefs of Staff to oversee short-term implementation and ensure that implementation plans meet the Secretary of Defense's first principle of retaining mission effectiveness.

If confirmed, will you ensure that all standards are realistic and preserve, or enhance, military readiness and mission capability?

Yes. I will ensure that all standards remain occupationally specific, operationally relevant, and in accordance with federal law. I will continue to support and monitor direction given to the Military Department Secretaries to require their respective Inspectors General to implement compliance inspection programs assessing whether their occupational standards – together with Service implementing methodologies – measure the combat readiness of combat units and are legally compliant.

The report of the Marine Corps' Ground Combat Exclusion Integrated Task Force reinforced other studies showing that female personnel experience injury rates in training that are two or three times greater than male personnel performing the same training.

In your view, can the prevalence of training injuries experienced by females be reduced without lowering overall physical requirements or standards? How could that be achieved?

Yes, I believe that by applying the myriad lessons we've already learned through four years of study and, by applying information gained as we implement, we can reduce the prevalence of training injuries for all Service members. DoD is a standards-based organization and will continue to be one.

The higher injury rates for female personnel may be further aggravated in sustained military service environments both in garrison while preparing for deployment, while deployed, and while conducting combat operations. In your view, can these injury rates be reduced or mitigated by redesign of military gear and equipment?

Yes, I believe military equipment should be closely examined to ensure injuries are not a result of improper fit or design. I fully support the June 26, 2015 guidance issued by the Under Secretary of Defense for Acquisition, Technology, and Logistics, which directed the Military Department Secretaries to take immediate steps to ensure combat equipment provided to female Service members is properly designed and fitted to accommodate their requirements, that it meets required standards for wear and survivability, and to continually monitor and address female sizing and fit issues in current and future combat equipment development and programs of record.

In your view, should combat loads for females be reduced to a level below that currently required of males to mitigate injury rates? If so, how would those reduced combat loads impact the combat readiness or effectiveness of small units to fight and win?

No. DoD is a standards-based organization and Service occupational standards are reflective of their operational requirements. Service members must meet the validated standards for a given occupation or position; any Service member who can meet those prescribed standards should be allowed to serve. Injury rates are being closely monitored by the Services and Special Operations Command.

In your view, is there a "critical mass" of female personnel required to effectively integrate combat arms units? If so, what do you believe would be the appropriate female-to-male composition necessary to achieve that critical mass?

I'm uncertain on this, and the matter deserves watching over the course of the next few years. The research on this question, as shown in many of the studies leading up to WISR, was tentative and inconclusive.

Selective Service Act

Some have suggested that the success of the All-Volunteer Force has reduced the need for our Nation to have a continuing authority and capability to conduct a draft. Further, a future national emergency may require that the military have the ability to identify citizens with unique and specialized skills to fill critical combat support requirements, both within the military and in the civilian sector. Currently, the Selective Service System does not identify individuals with such skills.

Do you believe the Selective Service Act should be repealed?

Given that the Armed Forces have waged the longest continuous conflict in our history with an All-Volunteer Force and the fact that all military career designators, occupational specialties, positions and units are now open to women, a review of the military selective service act is prudent. This is not solely a Defense issue, but rather part of a much broader national discussion.

Do you believe Congress should amend the Selective Service Act to require the registration of women?

The Selective Service Act should be reviewed, based on the recent experiences of the All-Volunteer Force and the fact that all military career designators, occupational specialties, and units are now open to women. This review should be part of a broad, national discussion. Moreover, I'd note that much of the conversation in the media thus far has addressed the question of whether to require women to register. I hope that the broader national conversation will include other options, such as repeal of the SSA, and entirely new models for conscription that leverage modern technology and realities, should we encounter such a national crisis.

Do you believe the Selective Service system, with its focus on supplying large numbers of replacement combat soldiers, meets the needs of today's military and the type of personnel that would likely need to be drafted in a future conflict, including skilled personnel in the medical, linguistic, cyber, and other specialist fields?

Given that the Armed Forces have waged the longest continuous conflict in our history with an All-Volunteer Force, a review of the military Selective Service Act is prudent.

But such a review must be part of a broader national discussion as this is not this solely a DoD issue.

The Selective Service system currently provides for alternate service, via the Selective Service Alternative Service Program for would-be draftees who profess to be conscientious objectors to any form of military service, non-military work that benefits the nation in the civilian sector, including in the areas of conservation, caring for the very young or old, education, and health care. Do you believe this provides a model for re-thinking Selective Service in this country to include addressing national security needs that reside outside of military service per se, and how we might best leverage the skills and abilities of the civilian population to address all national security needs (not just military) and other national goals?

Your question offers many of the same points of departure that should be considered in the greater national discussion concerning the future of the Selective Service system and continuation of registration. That conversation should include DoD's perspective, and I look forward to taking part in the discussion, but it has much broader implications regarding the needs of our nation.

Military Health Care Reform

The Department's FY17 TRICARE budget proposal would increase fees for beneficiaries. How does the Department plan to increase the value of the health benefit enough to balance the higher costs for beneficiaries?

Our beneficiaries want better access, more convenience, and a higher level of customer service. At the same time, we must ensure that our military medical providers maintain critical deployment related skills. The FY17 TRICARE budget is designed to ensure access for our beneficiaries at low to no cost and simultaneously encourage retirees to use our MTFs for care. In addition to our budget proposal we are undertaking a variety of administrative actions to add value and improve the beneficiaries' experience of care. Examples of these actions include: First call resolution for appointments; Implementing telehealth and other digital strategies to expand access to care; Ensuring that our system of care is safe and of the highest quality; and Removing any real or perceived barriers to care (example: not having to re-enroll when beneficiaries move into another managed care support contractor's region).

What is the Department's rationale for its proposal to charge enrollment fees for TRICARE For Life beneficiaries?

A modest enrollment fee for TRICARE for Life beneficiaries helps to balance the government/beneficiary proportional contributions to health care. The enrollment fees are structured to protect the most financially vulnerable, are grandfathered such that they will only apply to new TFL participants, and are far below what a typical Medicare-eligible beneficiary pays for a Medical supplemental plan.

14

What is the status of the pilot programs on urgent care and value-based provider reimbursement? When will those pilot programs begin?

It is my understanding that the Department is on track to meet the implementation deadlines for the urgent care and value-based provider reimbursement pilot programs of May 23, 2016.

In your view, what should the Services do to improve access to care in military medical facilities?

Working with Health Affairs, I will ensure that the appropriate resources are available to ensure access to care for beneficiaries and that we meet our access standards. I support using technology, as is done in the private sector, to provide alternatives for patients to engage their health care professionals.

In your view, what is the greatest threat to the long-term viability of the military health system?

The military health system is unique; we operate a global system of hospitals, clinics, and health team capabilities – both fixed and deployable –to meet the health needs of our military force, and to maintain the ability of our military medical professionals to support the full range of military operations. The number and capabilities of our hospitals and clinics, aeromedical evacuation assets, hospital ships, and other deployable medical capabilities, as well as the number and mix of active, reserve, and civilian medical personnel, are based on meeting the health readiness mission requirements first and foremost, and ensuring that our beneficiaries receive the health care they need. Over the last years of war, we fought as a joint force and we provided medical care in that joint environment. We must continually assess and modernize the way we execute mission to ensure long-term viability of the MHS.

Health Care Costs

If confirmed, what reforms in infrastructure, benefits, or benefit management would you implement to control the per capita costs of health care provided by the Department?

Our benefit reform proposal goes a long way towards equitably adjusting contributions for health care and achieving savings, which will reach about $1 billion per year. Part of our proposal will tie adjustments to participation fees and co-pays to a medical inflation rate, like National Health Expenditures, to ensure parity going forward. But we also see tremendous opportunity in incentives and enhancements to future TRICARE contracts, increased sharing with our close partner, the VA, and more operational efficiencies we see possible through the Shared Services we formed as part of the Defense Health Agency are top priorities. If confirmed, I will continue to aggressively pursue these and other opportunities to achieve greater efficiency and savings.

Autism Care Demonstration

One of the purposes of the Autism Care Demonstration (ACD) is to increase access and delivery of ABA services while creating a viable economic model. A RAND analysis warns that rates below commercial and public insurers "might lead providers either to leave TRICARE's networks or to prioritize Autism Spectrum Disorder children from other health insurers over TRICARE-covered children. Providers have expressed concerns that the proposed rate changes will fall far below market rates, and the rate reductions will result in service interruption in several locations and severely limit access to care nationally.

> In your view, will service interruption and access challenges (including delayed services or receiving less than prescribed levels of care) affect the overall results of the ACD?

TRICARE currently has one of the most robust autism care benefits in the nation. With all benefits covered by the catastrophic cap, and no preset limits on the amount of treatment provided, we are confident that military beneficiaries with autism will continue to have access to outstanding care. In addition, we lead the nation in quality initiatives in autism care, including supervision and certification requirements. The market for ABA services is dynamic, and I will personally review these rate changes to ensure that they do not have a negative effect on the ability for children within the TRICARE network to obtain the services they require.

> Did the Defense Health Agency performed an analysis of how many children currently served under the ACD will lose services or receive fewer services as a result of the published rate changes?

The current provider network is robust in most areas and our contractors are actively recruiting new providers. The revised rates were developed after two comprehensive external studies of comparable rates. According to these studies, TRICARE remains very competitive in the reimbursement amounts for ABA services. Of note, of the four rate structures proposed by the external studies, TRICARE adopted the one that provides the highest overall reimbursement levels. These rates come from a deliberate and thoughtful process on the part of the Department. Nevertheless, I plan to personally review this matter to ensure that all military children currently served under the ACD will continue to receive the services they need.

Service of Transgender Individuals

If confirmed, what would be your role in the review and approval of Department policy on whether transgender persons should be allowed to serve openly in the military, and what, if any, effect on health benefits such service may have?

If confirmed, I anticipate that I will to continue to lead the ongoing review directed by the Secretary of Defense of the policies impacting the service of transgender individuals and support the Secretary in implementing any policy changes that he might direct.

With respect to the medical care portion of the question, the Military Health System provides medically necessary care for Active Duty personnel for all health conditions. I am confident that will continue to be able to meet that standard, whatever decisions the Secretary makes on DoD policy regarding military service by transgender individuals.

Mental Health Care

If confirmed, what actions will you take to reduce the stigma associated with seeking mental health care by military personnel and their families?

If confirmed, I will build on the ongoing efforts to reduce the stigma associated with seeking mental health care and encourage the use of available resources among Service members and their families. This will include an integrated approach for continuing mental health research, prevention, and evidence-based treatment efforts that will allow the Department to provide high-quality, timely mental health services. I will also continue to work with the Departments of Veterans Affairs (VA) and Health and Human Services on our multiple interagency mental health initiatives for Service members, Veterans and their families. These include public awareness campaigns like DoD's "Real Warriors" and the VA's "Make the Connection" which encourage Service members to recognize the early signs of potential mental health issues and ask for help when they need it.

Do you believe that characterizing post-traumatic stress disorder as a disorder helps to create more stigma associated with this condition?

In ordinary conversation, I think it is better to talk about "post-traumatic stress" rather than "post-traumatic stress disorder." "Post-traumatic stress disorder" is the term used by the medical and mental health provider community to classify the clinical diagnosis of PTSD, but the Department recognizes that that "post-traumatic stress" exists on a continuum and does not in all cases constitute a "disorder." As a result, medical jargon might differ from non-medical terminology.

We are engaged on multiple levels to decrease the stigma associated with seeking counseling for post-traumatic stress at any level of severity. The Department has undertaken several major policy and program changes in this area, such as co-locating mental health providers in primary care clinics and limiting the circumstances in which command notification of mental health treatment is required. Embedding mental health

17

providers in close proximity with line units improves access, continuity of care, and also reduces stigma. As a result, Army utilization of outpatient mental healthcare has increased from approximately 900,000 encounters in FY07 to approximately 2 million in FY15. Additionally, between 2011 and 2015, the Department funded the training of 2,769 mental health providers in evidence-based psychotherapies for PTSD. With more Service members receiving counseling and care in outpatient and non-clinical settings, mental health conditions, including post-traumatic stress, are being managed earlier and often before crises occur.

In your view, are DOD's current mental health resources adequate to serve all active duty and eligible reserve component members and their families, as well as retirees and their dependents?

In recent years, the Department has undertaken significant efforts to increase and improve the mental health resources available to Service members, their families, and retirees. For example, since 2009, the Department increased the number of mental health professionals providing care to Service members, retirees and their families by 42% (to 9,295). The number of network behavioral health facilities also increased from approximately 914 in 2013 to 1,757 in 2015. The Department has also implemented embedded care models in recent years that have shifted providers from traditional hospital settings into operational units or satellite clinics in close proximity to where Service members work.

For Guard and Reserve Service members and their families, in addition to care provided while on an active duty status, multiple non-clinical counseling programs are available, including the *inTransition* program, where we are calling every separating Service member with an identified mental health issue to facilitate their transition to VA, TRICARE or community mental health care as needed. The reserve component also has access to Military OneSource, the Yellow Ribbon Reintegration Program, and other education and outreach programs. These programs identify and refer those in need of more intensive clinical mental health services. For active duty dependents, retirees and their dependents, the Department recently published a proposed rule on TRICARE Mental Health and Substance Use Disorder Treatment that will substantially expand mental health and substance use disorder treatment services, cover new types of mental health treatment programs, and reduce overall administrative barriers to access inpatient and residential mental health treatment when needed.

In light of recent studies by RAND and the GAO (which predate our efforts listed above), however, if confirmed I will direct a review of access to mental health care and assess where demand exceeds available mental health resources and how we can use our mental health provider workforce more efficiently and effectively.

Suicide Prevention

The numbers of suicides in each of the Services continues to be of great concern to the Committee. The Defense Suicide Prevention Office was established in November 2011, to oversee the strategic development, implementation, centralization, standardization, communication and evaluation of DOD suicide and risk reduction programs, policies and surveillance activities.

What is your view of the effectiveness of the suicide prevention programs overseen by the Defense Suicide Prevention Office?

We recognize that when a Service member dies from suicide, it is rarely due to "one" reason. As a result, prevention efforts have to be both comprehensive and evidence-based. Over the past year, the Services, in concert with the Defense Suicide Prevention Office, have made great strides in implementing evidence-based practices that are effective at identifying Service members at risk and getting them into care. For example, the Services have established bystander intervention training programs that teach Service members to recognize the risks and warning signs of suicide and how to intervene in a caring manner. Additionally, since we understand that our suicide deaths often coincide with relationship, financial or legal struggles, there are a host of effective, non-medical, community based programs aimed at helping those that are struggling with these very issues. While I know that our current efforts are effective, they are not enough, and we continue our efforts to learn and improve.

If confirmed, do you have plans to enhance these suicide prevention programs?

Yes, through continued development of a comprehensive research strategy aimed at closing our knowledge gaps and expanding the Services' use of evidenced-based programs, we will continue to learn and adjust our approaches to addressing this very complex and important issue.

What is your view of the effectiveness of the Defense Suicide Prevention Office in overseeing these programs?

The Defense Suicide Prevention Office has provided a critical coordination and oversight capability. The expertise in this office has been fundamental in identifying which, of many previously existing programs, are evidence-based and should be shared among the Services, and in coordinating and facilitating a comprehensive research strategy to identify and address our knowledge gaps in the Department.

If confirmed, what role would you play in shaping Department of Defense policies to help prevent suicides both in garrison and in theater and to increase the resiliency of all service members and their families?

The recent enterprise reorganization of the Office of the Under Secretary of Defense for Personnel and Readiness created the Office of the Executive Director for Force

Resiliency, whose mission is to strengthen and promote the resiliency and readiness of the Total Force. The offices within Force Resiliency include the Defense Suicide Prevention Office, as well as the Sexual Assault and Prevention Office, the Office of Diversity Management and Equal Opportunity, Personnel Risk Reduction, and the Office for DoD and VA Collaboration. With this new Directorate, I will increase the synergy and collaboration of resiliency efforts and identify comprehensive resiliency indicators and reporting systems to ensure we have a highly resilient military force.

Voluntary Education Programs

The Department continues to seek ways to improve oversight of its tuition assistance programs, including standardizing eligibility criteria among the Services and requiring all schools who accept tuition assistance funding, whether for online courses or on-post, to sign a Memorandum of Understanding with the Department which will, among other things, subject online schools to Departmental audits.

What is your assessment of the tuition assistance program in light of the needs of the Services and the current budget environment?

The Department places high value on programs designed to support professional and personal development as well as the successful transition of our Service members to the civilian workforce. Even in a time of constrained budgets and resources, DoD manages a Tuition Assistance Program that maximizes education benefits for Service members and helps them achieve significant personal and professional goals. In fiscal year 2015, Tuition Assistance funds supported over 286,000 Service members enrolled in more than 760,000 postsecondary courses. If confirmed, I will continue the work with the Services to meet the needs of the Total Force by sustaining the appropriate level of resources for this program.

What is your view of tuition assistance as a transition benefit for service members to obtain civilian licenses and credentials?

Tuition Assistance (TA) is a very valuable tool in assisting Service members to earn civilian licenses and credentials prior to separation from military service. TA can be used to pay for academic coursework that supports earning a credential or licensure when part of an approved academic degree plan. Furthermore, earning a professional credential or license broadens Service members' occupational knowledge and furthers their contribution to the military "profession of arms." If confirmed, I look forward to working with the Military Departments to increase opportunities for Service members to use their Tuition Assistance productively, to benefit the individual service member and his or her transition, as well as the greater mission.

What is your view of proposed changes to the so-called 90/10 rule that would require academic institutions to derive no more than 85 percent of their revenue from federal sources, including DOD tuition assistance and VA GI Bill funding?

While DoD has no objection to the proposal to include Title 10 Tuition Assistance funds in the Federal portion of the 90/10 calculation, any statutory changes to the proposed 90/10 rule would likely reside with the Department of Education.

What is your view on for-profit educational institutions that provide educational services at a higher tuition rate than public universities having the same access to DOD tuition assistance and VA GI Bill funding?

Whether the Service member selects a program of study that is offered online or in the classroom, with a private or public institution, the Tuition Assistance program enables funding up to $250 per semester hour toward that member's education-related goal. The Department's Tuition Assistance program intentionally enables a wide array of educational opportunities to support the many and varied needs of our military students. If confirmed, I will continue to work with educational institutions providing meaningful information to students about the financial cost of attendance at an institution so our military students can make informed decisions on where to attend school.

Do you believe that educational institutions should have to prove their success rates of placing students into jobs before obtaining DOD tuition assistance and VA GI Bill funding?

The Department supports the gainful employment regulations that reside with the Department of Education. In fact, DoD policy requires educational institutions that wish to participate in the DoD Tuition Assistance Program be certified to participate in Department of Education's Title IV, Federal Student Aid programs prior to an educational institution receiving funds from a service's Tuition Assistance program. If confirmed, I will continue to work with the Department of Education in enforcing its gainful employment protections with respect to our military students.

Department of Defense Instruction (DoDI) 1322.25 does not provide administrative procedures for the fair and expeditious adjudication of complaints about educational institutions that have entered into a memorandum of understanding (MOU) with DOD for a Voluntary Education Partnership. As a result, there is no clear guidance on the rights and responsibilities of the DOD or of the educational institution prior to and following a DOD decision to suspend or terminate a MOU.

If confirmed, what action would you take to ensure that the Department of Defense implements administrative procedures adequate for the fair and expeditious adjudication of complaints about educational institutions that have entered into an MOU with DOD for a Voluntary Education Partnership?

Safeguarding Service member access to quality post-secondary education is a strategic investment that supports mission accomplishment and successful transition to civilian life. As such, I take complaints about educational institutions seriously. When there are violations of Department agreements, MOUs and policies, the Department takes appropriate action. The DoD Instruction 1322.25, "Voluntary Education Programs," clearly articulates the circumstances by which an MOU may be cancelled, terminated, or suspended to include basic notification and appeal processes. If confirmed, I will continue to communicate our standardized processes and procedures to review and decide what action is appropriate when we are in receipt of reports of non-compliance with the DoD Voluntary Education Partnership MOU.

Defense Department Civilian Vacancies

Until recently, you were serving in an acting position that appears to violate the Federal Vacancies Reform Act of 1998 (FVRA). Under title 5, United States Code section 3348(d), an action taken by any person whose appointment is not in compliance with FVRA shall have no force or effect and may not be ratified.

Do you believe that your acting appointment was in violation of the FVRA? If not, why not?

I understand that my service as the Acting Under Secretary of Defense for Personnel and Readiness followed the consistent interpretation of the Federal Vacancies Reform Act of 1998 by Administrations of both parties since the Act was passed. I also understand that this is a matter in litigation and that consequently it would be inappropriate to comment further.

If so, what actions, if any, did you take to communicate the FVRA violation to the Secretary of Defense?

Please see above response.

Provide a complete description of all actions you took while in an acting capacity in violation of the FVRA that may be without force and effect.

Please see above response.

Religious Accommodations

On July 22, 2015 the Department of Defense Inspector General released a report on "Rights of Conscience Protections for Armed Forces Service Members and Their Chaplains." The Inspector General found that the services are not processing special religious accommodation requests promptly and, once accommodation requests are approved, they do not last for the duration of soldiers' military careers. In many cases, this has put individuals in the difficult position of being forced to violate their faith in order to join the military and they must resubmit accommodation requests every time they transfer military bases. In some cases, these policies are unfairly burdening individuals specifically recruited by our armed forces for their unique language, culture, and technical skills.

If confirmed, what would be your role in addressing the recommendations in the Inspector General report?

I would continue the process already underway of establishing new policy that addresses the areas for improvement identified in the Inspector General's report.

Do you support a policy to allow service members' religious accommodations to follow their service throughout their entire military careers – no matter where they are stationed?

I support a policy pursuant to which religious accommodations afforded to a Service member will continue – until and unless – "there is a compelling government interest that requires withdrawal of that accommodation." If confirmed, I will continue the work already underway, to update current DoD policies in this regard.

Do you support a policy that would allow prospective recruits to request accommodation prior to enlisting or accepting a commission for service in the armed forces?

If confirmed, I would continue the process, already underway, of establishing new policy that addresses the areas for improvement identified in the Inspector General's report.

American military personnel routinely deploy to locations around the world where they must engage and work effectively with allies and host-country nationals whose faiths and beliefs may be different than their own. For many other cultures, religious faith is not a purely personal and private matter; it is the foundation of their culture and society. Learning to respect the different faiths and beliefs of others, and to understand how accommodating different views can contribute to a diverse force is, some would argue, an essential skill to operational effectiveness.

In your view, do policies concerning religious accommodation in the military appropriately accommodate the free exercise of religion and other beliefs, including individual expressions of belief, without impinging on those who have different beliefs, including no religious belief?

Yes.

In your view, does a military climate that welcomes and respects open and candid discussions about personal religious faith and beliefs in a garrison environment contribute in a positive way to preparing U.S. forces to be effective in overseas assignments? Would a policy that discourages open discussions about personal faith and beliefs be more or less effective at preparing service members to work and operate in a pluralistic environment?

Current Department policy places a "high value on the rights of members of the Military Services to observe the tenets of their respective religions or to observe no religion at all," neither encouraging nor discouraging discussions of religion by individual Service members. I believe our current policy wisely balances individual rights and military readiness.

Force of the Future

The Committee has been conducting a series of hearings on reforming the Department of Defense. A number of witnesses have called for reforms to the Pentagon's personnel management system to ensure we recruit and retain the best and the brightest to work for the nation's defense. This Committee is concerned, however, that on an issue of such importance, the Pentagon has chosen not to consult the Congress in its deliberations, yet foreign military officials, think tanks, and union representatives have received detailed briefings on Force of the Future (FOTF) that have not been provided to the Congress.

What was your role, if any, in establishing and executing the FOTF initiative?

When I was re-assigned to the Office of the Under Secretary of Defense for Personnel and Readiness, Secretary Carter had already announced his Force of the Future initiative at his former high school in Abington, Pennsylvania. Shortly thereafter, I provided a memorandum which outlined, in broad terms, how his vision might be realized and what I viewed as the general challenges that our military and civilian personnel systems faced. Secretary Carter then directed me to execute a plan in accordance with my memorandum to him. From that point forward, I served as Secretary Carter's principal agent and executor on the Force of the Future initiative and assembled a small research and writing team to assist me. Working Groups within the Department had already been established and I began chairing those sessions as they developed reform proposal ideas and possible options for implementation. I personally oversaw the development of reform proposal ideas, provided guidance and direction to the research and writing team, and approved the final set of reform proposals that we presented to the Deputy Secretary of Defense in August 2015.

What role, if any, did you have in briefs to foreign military officials, think tanks, and union representatives prior to public announcement of the FOTF initiative?

I personally discussed the Force of the Future initiative, in broad terms, with the Chief of General Staff and a Minister of the Armed Forces from the UK, discussed the proposed reforms with leadership from both RAND and Institute for Defense Analyses (IDA) based on their extensive pre-existing research on military and civilian personnel reform, and personally met with the leadership of unions that requested meetings with me to address their concerns after v2.0 of the reform proposals was leaked publically.

What are the clearly defined problems faced by the current military personnel system that the FOTF initiative is aimed at addressing?

As the Secretary of Defense has publically stated, the Force of the Future initiative was developed to focus on ways in which the Department could increase permeability of personnel and ideas between the public and private sector, increase recruiting results and outcomes for the Department, and emphasize talent management and retention to ensure that the quality of today's current force will translate to a "Force of the Future."

Additionally, the Secretary has also approved reform proposals focused on improving the quality of life of military parents so they may better balance commitments they make to serve in uniform and start and support a family. Secretary Carter believes this comprehensive package of family benefits will enable the Department to attract, incentivize, and retain the best talent today and in the future.

What actions, if any, has the Department taken to determine whether the FOTF proposals would address those problems?

The Secretary has already approved more than three dozen reform initiatives of the 81 presented to him in August 2015. Many required significant study and analysis in their formulation; more still, before the Secretary was convinced that they would appropriately address the problem areas he identified and that I have already mentioned elsewhere in these answers. The Military Services and certain components within the Office of the Secretary of Defense (OSD) have already submitted initial implementation plans for the initiatives announced by the Secretary in November 2015 and those plans are currently under initial review. To my knowledge, the only initiatives that are currently being actively implemented across the Department are expanded Maternity Leave and the creation of the Defense Digital Service (DDS).

Military Pay and Allowances

The Department has traditionally compared Regular Military Compensation against comparable civilian salaries to devise a percentile as a way to assess the relative attractiveness of military pay versus civilian pay.

What is the current comparable percentile of military pay versus civilian pay for officers and enlisted personnel?

A 2012 study (2009 data) found that military compensation compares favorably with private sector wages for American workers of similar education/experience and that on average, enlisted personnel are paid at the 90th percentile and officers are paid at the 83rd percentile relative to their civilian counterparts.

How do these percentiles compare to the base level at which the Department feels military compensation must be to effectively recruit and retain the highest quality personnel possible for military service?

The Department's base level of the 70th percentile was set in a study produced almost 15 years ago. We have started a study of the base level of Regular Military Compensation to ensure it remains a relevant comparator for today's military force and expect those results this summer. The Department continually monitors the competitiveness of military compensation to ensure it remains sufficient to recruit and retain the high-quality force we need today and into the future.

What is your assessment of the current military basic pay table in terms of providing adequate and competitive pay for military members and their families?

The current military basic pay table remains adequate, competitive, and sufficient to recruit and retain the high-quality force we need today. We are reviewing the pay table to determine whether it is properly aligned with the Department's talent management needs for the future force.

What changes, if any, would you recommend for the revision of the military pay table?

I do not have any changes to recommend at this time, but, if confirmed, I will continue to closely monitor this critical issue and make recommendations for changes that I believe are appropriate.

In a recent hearing concerning military personnel reform one witness recommended flexible authorities for the military departments to establish career and retirement packages that recognize the different professional qualifications within the services. It was suggested that military career lengths be extended beyond thirty years of service for military specialties such as medical and legal, and perhaps shorter careers for infantry and similar combat arms positions.

What is your view on the need for such flexibilities?
The Department needs a broad range of authorities, personnel policies, and military compensation strategies that are flexible enough to address recruiting and retention issues that arise over time in a wide variety of career fields. The Department is reviewing whether current mandatory retirement ages continue to meet the needs of the joint force.

If needed, what changes would you advocate to the military pay tables and to the military compensation and retirement system to achieve any desired flexibility?

Thanks to the efforts of the Congress, the Department is currently implementing one of the most significant changes to the military retirement system in generations, which will provide the Department and members with a modernized and more flexible retirement system. I do not have any additional changes to recommend at this time. While the current military basic pay table is competitive and sufficient to recruit and retain the high-quality force we need today, the Department is reviewing the pay table and other elements of military compensation to determine whether they are properly aligned with the Department's talent management needs for tomorrow's force.

The Senate-passed version of the National Defense Authorization Act for Fiscal Year 2016 included a provision that would restore the original purpose of the Basic Allowance for Housing, to provide a tax-exempt allowance for military members and their families to purchase or lease adequate private housing. This provision addressed the situation in which two or more military members form a household where each receives a Basic Allowance for Housing. It was included with an Administration proposal to reduce Basic Allowance for Housing rates to provide an up to 5% out of pocket contribution by military members to their private housing, based on market rates.

What are your views on whether the Basic Allowance for Housing should be provided to all military members comprising a single household?

I support the purpose of the Basic Allowance for Housing as a fundamental part of Regular Military Compensation provided to all members, regardless of members' household choices. If I am confirmed, I will continue to review the Basic Allowance for Housing and make recommendations for changes that I believe are appropriate to maintain the competitiveness of Regular Military Compensation with private sector compensation.

If the Basic Allowance for Housing is considered part of compensation rather than an allowance, particularly for those households that receive two or more Basic Allowances for Housing, should it be taxed as ordinary income?   Should it be included in the calculation of retired pay?

It is my view that the Basic Allowance for Housing should not be taxed. Taxing this allowance would reduce the amount of the allowance that members have to pay for housing in their local areas, and may preclude them from being able to obtain suitable, adequate housing for their paygrade with the remainder. The recent enactment of a new retirement system for the military is a significant and meaningful change to military compensation. Making a further change to include BAH as part of the retirement calculation would require additional analysis to understand the full impact.
If I am confirmed, I will review this matter and make recommendations for changes that I believe are appropriate.

How would you amend the current system of allowances to provide adequate housing for all members of the military while also providing pay that is sufficiently competitive with that of civilian counterparts of comparable age and educational attainment?

Regular Military Compensation today compares favorably with private sector wages for American workers of similar education/experience. At this time, I do not see a need to amend these programs. However, if I am confirmed, I would review military compensation and make recommendations for changes that I believe are appropriate.

Do the military pay tables adequately compensate individuals for their specialized skills and provide an incentive to recruit science and engineering professionals into the military?

The military basic pay tables and the special and incentive pay authorities provided by the Congress do provide the ability to efficiently target additional compensation to individuals with specialized skills. The Department is reviewing the pay table and other elements of military compensation to determine whether they are properly aligned with the Department's talent management needs for tomorrow's force. If I am confirmed, I will continue this review and make recommendations for changes that I believe are appropriate. The Department is also, through the Force of the Future and other initiatives, pursuing non-monetary means of recruiting and retaining the best talent, to include those in technical fields.

If confirmed, would you advocate for a review of the adequacy of military pay tables?

The Department is reviewing the pay table and other elements of military compensation to determine whether they are properly aligned with the Department's talent management needs for tomorrow's force.

Readiness Responsibilities

Section 136 of title 10, United States Code, gives the Under Secretary of Defense for Personnel and Readiness certain responsibilities for military readiness. Some important issues that affect military readiness, however, such as logistics and materiel readiness, have been placed under the jurisdiction of the Under Secretary for Acquisition, Technology, and Logistics.

In your view, what are the most significant challenges to the current readiness of our Armed Forces?

Currently, I'm concerned that unpredictable funding levels will thwart the Services' efforts to recover full spectrum readiness in the coming years in order to successfully meet the tenets of the defense strategy. In addition to stable funding levels, the Services require time to recover readiness; the global demand for our operations and capabilities strains the Services' ability to recover and train at home following 14 years of combat.

Readiness for high-end, high tech conflict demands a markedly different skill set than the counterinsurgency skills we've honed over the two wars. The Services continue to shift from counterinsurgency-focused training to training that addresses high-end contingency, full spectrum warfighter requirements, but require time and predictable funding to get there.

What is your understanding of the term, "Readiness" as it applies to the responsibilities of the Under Secretary of Defense for Personnel and Readiness?

I define readiness as the Department's ability to deploy and generate adequately manned, trained and equipped forces required to execute the missions assigned by the President. This involves assessing and advising the Secretary on the state of military readiness, total force management (Active Component and Reserve Component), and the global allocation of our forces to ensure efficient and effective support of wartime and peacetime operations, contingency planning and preparedness. In partnership with the Office of the Chairman of the Joint Chiefs of Staff and the Armed Forces, it will be my primary duty to develop policies, plans and programs to ensure we have the right type and number of ready forces required to meet the demands of the National Military Strategy.

In your view, is it necessary that the responsibilities of the Under Secretary of Defense for Personnel and Readiness with respect to Readiness be assigned to this position? Why or why not? If not, to what other officer or official of the Department, the Joint Staff, or the military departments should the Readiness responsibilities be assigned?

There have been numerous studies on how to measure and define the readiness of our force, and one finding is invariably conclusive: the quality of our people is the hallmark of what makes the U.S. military the pre-eminent global fighting force. As such, the health of our all-volunteer force, analyzed though qualitative and quantitative metrics through other offices in the Under Secretariat, is inextricably linked to the readiness we need to execute the defense strategy. In fact, the importance of understanding strategic readiness within an increasingly unpredictable global landscape is evidenced by the Department's recent decision to elevate readiness oversight and management to the Assistant Secretary of Defense level. We should and will continue to work closely with the Services and Joint Staff to create synergies and define roles and responsibilities in managing readiness across the Department.

What is your assessment of the impacts and challenges to DOD readiness as a result of sequestration?

It is my understanding that degraded readiness levels are largely attributed to prolonged counterinsurgency-based combat operations. The cuts posed by sequestration exacerbated already existing problems, undermined the Services' plans to recover full-spectrum readiness, and forced the Department to make hard choices to balance current and future readiness. The Force continues to be stressed in meeting operational demand globally, but the Services are able to meet the minimum operational requirements. The brunt of sequestration's effects was felt most in our ability to generate forces to meet contingency surge requirements—our readiness for major wars. Some of these effects will take considerable time and predictable resources to reverse.

What is your assessment of the current readiness of our Armed Forces to execute the Defense Strategic Guidance?

Today our ready forces are postured globally, conducting counter-terrorism, stability, and deterrence operations. They maintain a stabilizing presence, conduct bilateral and multilateral training to burden-share and enhance our security relationships, and provide the crisis response capabilities required to protect U.S. National Security interests and deter potential adversaries from major conflict. While we remain able to meet the demand of current operations and the steady state requirements that the nation asks of us, persistent operational demand and fiscal instability have made readiness recovery more challenging. While the specifics should be discussed in a classified environment, our ability to generate the surge required for a high-end emergent crisis is a very real and serious concern as we recover full spectrum readiness following operations in Iraq and Afghanistan.

What is your understanding of the responsibilities of the Under Secretary of Defense for Personnel and Readiness and relationship to the Assistant Secretary of Defense for Logistics and Materiel Readiness in ensuring military readiness, including materiel readiness?

It is my understanding that the responsibilities of the USD (P&R) are to develop policies, plans, and programs for the Total Force to ensure efficient and effective support of wartime and peacetime operations, contingency planning, and preparedness whereas the Assistant Secretary of Defense for Logistics and Materiel Readiness (ASD L&MR) oversees materiel readiness which supports operational readiness. With Service readiness challenges largely distributed along personnel, training and equipment challenges, if confirmed, I envision heavy partnership with ASD L&MR in managing policy and readiness oversight in all aspects of equipping and supporting our force.

What are the most critical objectives to improve readiness reporting and monitoring of the military forces, and if confirmed, how would you work with the Military Departments as well as other Office of the Secretary of Defense offices to achieve them?

To understand readiness, we must be successful in two areas. First, we must collect the right data—timely, accurate, and relevant information about the supply and demand for ready forces. This is an analytical challenge—we currently do this well, and are committed to improving further still. Second, no less of a challenge, we must understand what the data means—how it weighs on the serious questions of strategy, risk, and resourcing tradeoffs that the Secretary and Chairman must answer. I'm committed to partnering with the Departments, Joint Staff, Combatant Commands, and OSD offices to advance in both areas.

Regarding partnerships, we must ensure we're vectored on the correct metrics from the tactical, joint, and strategic levels that inform us about our ability to answer the National Military Strategy. This means working effectively with OSD (Policy), Joint Staff and the Military Departments. Additionally, it is essential to be able to monitor not just the status of unit readiness but the health of the pipelines that drive and support that readiness. These downstream metrics not only provide a more complete picture of readiness, but they are also the key to forecasting problems.

End Strength Reductions

In 2014, the Department proposed a defense strategy that included eventual end strengths of 450,000 for the Army and 182,000 for the Marine Corps over the subsequent five years.

What is your understanding of the Army's and Marine Corps' ability to meet these goals without forcing out many soldiers and marines who have served in combat over the past 15 years with the implicit promise that they could compete for career service and retirement?

The Army and Marine Corps have indicated they will meet their prescribed end strengths on schedule. All of the Services have worked hard to affect the drawdown with minimal involuntary separations, while ensuring we retain needed quality and combat experience.

What programs are in place to ensure that separating and retiring service members are as prepared as they can be as they reenter the civilian economy?

In partnership with the Department of Veterans Affairs, Department of Labor, Department of Education, Small Business Administration, and the Office of Personnel Management, the DoD has redesigned the Transition Assistance Program (TAP) to prepare all Service members, both Active and Reserve Component, for employment, attending an institution of higher learning or career technical training program, or starting a business. TAP includes service member counseling and training sessions, employment and career workshops, and education opportunities throughout the military life cycle, all while maintaining leadership focus on, and involvement in, each service member's transition process. DoD provides opportunities for service member credentialing and job skills training prior to separation.

What steps are being taken to offer reserve billets to active duty members being involuntarily separated due to the drawdown?

As part of their transition programs, all of the Services encourage eligible active duty members who are separating to consider continuing their service as members of the Reserve Components. This portion of the transition program has received renewed emphasis as part of Service drawdown plans.

How fast can the Army and Marine Corps responsibly and fairly reduce end strength while maintaining the integrity and readiness of combat units?

The Army and Marine Corps will continue to implement significant reductions over the next several years, but at a pace that responsibly ensures their ability to make ready the force they have now and in the future. The Marine Corps will meet its goal of 182,000 active duty in FY 17 and the Army will meet its end-strength goal of 980,000 Active, Guard and Reserve Soldiers in FY 18. Our military must remain able to respond to any large-scale contingency operation. This will require careful consideration on the part of the Services about their organizational structures and their ability to reconstitute and mobilize forces.

If sequestration continues through 2018, what will be the impact on the active duty and reserve end strengths of all the services, and how would the mix between the active and reserve forces be affected?

The continuation of sequestration will have a significant negative impact on the Department's ability to perform its missions, and may necessitate continued adjustments to end-strength levels for both our active and reserve components. If confirmed, I will support the Services as they strive to achieve the best possible levels and mix of military end-strength.

What is your understanding of the need for additional force shaping tools requiring legislation beyond what Congress has provided?

Through the Force of the Future initiative, if confirmed, I hope to work with Congress to pursue flexibility within DOPMA, the new retirement system, and other tools that serve both retention and force shaping goals.

Recruiting and Retention

The Department of Defense has indicated that approximately 25 percent of today's youth population is eligible for military service. This number is alarmingly low.

What are the main reasons for such a small pool of individuals in the 17-24 years of age population being eligible for service? Do you believe the current standards for enlistment are the right standards?

Although the Department continues to recruit the best and the brightest of America's young adults to sustain the All-Volunteer Force, our latest information indicates that unfortunately, only 29 percent of today's youth meet the standards for military service without a waiver. The majority of these disqualifications result from obesity and other medical conditions. Today's enlistment standards are appropriate, allowing the Services to accomplish their missions by recruiting a diverse force drawn from the best of today's youth.

What is your view of the importance of increasing the number individuals for service that are older than the typical core recruiting demographic?

Anticipating the recruiting environment will continue to become more challenging, it is important for the Department and the Services to continuously identify ways to expand the pool of eligible individuals. Expanding that pool to older recruits is an option that may be considered, provided it will not impact the high quality expected of our new recruits.

Some services have recently relaxed grooming and appearance standards. In your view, how will this impact recruiting and retention?

The Services frequently review, and as appropriate, make changes to these policies in accordance with their individual needs. I am committed, if confirmed, to working with the Services to ensure that any proposed adjustments to these standards are carefully reviewed to ensure our full understanding of the implications such modifications may have, including their potential impact on recruiting and retention.

As the economy continues to recover and strengthen, what is your assessment of the current recruiting climate? What legislative authorities, if any, do you believe would be helpful to improve recruiting?

As the economy continues to improve, the Department is starting to encounter a more challenging recruiting environment. Currently, we are well positioned to ensure near-term success in recruiting. We have an ongoing effort studying whether additional legislative authority is needed to ensure that we are best positioned to recruit in the longer term.

Given the shrinking eligible population combined with the current force structure drawdowns and strengthening economy, do you believe the Department is, or soon will be, facing a recruiting and retention issue?

Despite today's challenges, the Department is achieving our recruiting goals. There are indicators, however, that the growing economy, the shrinking population of youth qualified for military service, the decreasing population of youth propensed to serve, and budgetary pressures will challenge the Services in recruiting and retaining the best and most qualified Service members. These realities remain a significant and constant concern.

What policies or tools are needed by the Department to increase the propensity to serve of today's youth?

Your continued support, together with that of other members in Congress, is essential to maintaining adequate investments in recruiting resources, which will generate the future force upon which the nation will depend. Specifically, I would ask that you consider how the Congress might broaden the means by which we approach America's youth. Mass marketing in traditional media, as well as more tailored social media campaigns will provide increased opportunities to afford both young Americans and their influencers (e.g., parents, teachers and coaches, clergy) access to accurate information about military service. The best way to improve propensity is to improve the perception of what it means to serve. Providing the Department the necessary flexibility to execute marketing, advertising and outreach programs in a manner that allows each Service to bridge knowledge gaps, correct misperceptions and reinforce a consistent, positive message is essential to sustaining the All-Volunteer Force.

Military Accessions Vital to National Interest Program

Under the Military Accessions Vital to National Interest (MAVNI) program, the Services may recruit non-permanent resident aliens who have certain high-demand medical or linguistic skills for service in the armed forces, and offer them an expedited path to citizenship.

What is the status of the MAVNI program?

The MAVNI pilot program, started in 2008 and continued with several adjustments and extensions, remains an active pilot program that recruits individuals whose enlistments are determined to be vital to the national interest. DoD utilizes this program to recruit and fill critical needs for qualified health care professionals and people with certain language and associated culture capabilities. The program is due to end in October of 2016, but the Department is examining the Services' needs for an extension. I will, if confirmed, ensure review and oversight of this pilot.

How many individuals have been recruited under the program since its restart, and in what occupations?

The Military Services utilize the MAVNI authority to recruit and fill critical needs for qualified health care professionals and people with certain language and associated culture capabilities. Since reinstatement on May 16, 2012, there have been 5,092 MAVNI accessions.

- FY 13 - 1,134 (1,088 language/46 health care providers)
- FY 14 - 1,303 (1,202 language/101 health care providers)
- FY 15 - 2,655 (2,622 language/33 health care providers)

In Fiscal Year 2015, Army, the primary user of the MAVNI authority, contracted 1,640 Regular Army enlistments, 981 Army Reserve enlistment and 33 health care professionals (HCPs). The majority of these new enlistments were for the top five MAVNI languages: Korean (544); Chinese (370); Nepalese (173); French (88); and

Tagalog (81) for Regular Army. The Army Reserve's top five languages were Nepalese (216); Korean (211); Chinese (191); Hindi (106) and Yoruba (48). The remainder of the Active and Reserve Component MAVNI enlistments is spread across several other languages.

There were 337 Army applicants (247 - Active / 90 – Reserve Component) with DACA (Deferred Action for Childhood Arrivals) authorization in the Army Delayed Entry Pool (DEP). Only 9 (2%) have received a favorably adjudicated Single-Scope Background Investigation (SSBI), as required for all MAVNI applicants. The average SSBI takes approximately 8 months to complete. Five DACA recipients have shipped to Basic Training. The top DACA Languages (both Active and Reserve Component) are: Korean (250), Tagalog (30), Portuguese (19) and Chinese (11). The remaining 27 enlistments are from various languages.

Of the 33 HCPs, 29 of them are Army Reserve physicians: Dentists (13); Psychiatrists (4); Anesthesiologists and Family Medicine Physicians (3 each); General Surgeons (2); and Entomologist, Emergency Medicine Physician, OBGYN and Internal Medicine Physician (1 each). The Reserve Component accessed 4 Internal Medicine Physicians

The Air Force accessed one MAVNI from Kenya who is fluent in Swahili.

What is your view of expanding the scope of the program to include more traditional, less specialized occupations, and to increasing the number of individuals that may be recruited under the program?

Expansion of the MAVNI program beyond critical skill sets to include less specialized occupations would require a change in law. Section 504 of Title 10 is clear that individual enlistments must be based on the "vital" requirement.

Mobilization and Demobilization of National Guard and Reserves

Over the past 14 years, the National Guard and Reserves have experienced their largest and most sustained employment since World War II. Reserve force management policies and systems have been characterized in the past as "inefficient and rigid" and readiness levels have been adversely affected by equipment stay-behind, cross-leveling, and reset policies.

What is your assessment of advances made in improving reserve component mobilization and demobilization procedures, and in what areas do problems still exist?

Over the past fourteen years, the Department has implemented policy changes governing the utilization of the Guard and Reserves and expanded pre- and post-mobilization benefits for active duty periods. These improvements have served to enhance predictability and morale among Service members. The Department strives to provide timely access to the Reserve Components and to mitigate any adverse impact on members back at home or in their jobs. Ensuring or reducing the potential for adverse impacts due to deployments on individual members of the Reserve Component is an area I will continue to assess.

What do you consider to be the most significant enduring changes to the administration of the reserve components aimed at ensuring their readiness for future mobilization requirements?

Significant enduring changes include Title 10 Section 12304b mobilization authority provided by the Congress in the FY 2012 NDAA, which enables continued focus on readiness and Reserve Component utilization for non-named contingencies. Other enduring features include the exceptional Reserve Component performance record and support of the American people and employers. If confirmed, I will look to the RC in order to determine where its use aids the readiness of the Total Force.

Do you see a need to modify current statutory authorities for the mobilization of members of the National Guard and Reserves?

The Department is evaluating some minor adjustments to current authorities that will provide improved use of the Reserve Components. One example is the Department's request to improve 12304b by allowing the Services to use Reserve Components for Service-unique missions. Currently under 12304b, Reserve Components can only be used for COCOM mission sets. If confirmed I will continue to assess this issue and request additional or modified authorities if I conclude they are necessary.

What is your assessment of the Department of Defense programs to assist members of the National Guard and Reserves as they transition from a mobilized status?

As a Reservist myself who served in Iraq, I can tell you that predictability and open communications are two key elements in the sustainment of readiness and morale of Reserve Component Service members and their families. Since 2008, the Yellow Ribbon Reintegration Program (YRRP) has provided invaluable deployment and reintegration support for the Reserve Components. Its efforts, in collaboration with partners like Employer Support of the Guard and Reserve, Transition GPS (Goals, Plans, Success), the Department of Veterans Affairs and the community-based network of care, provide information, access, referrals and outreach to military members, their families, employers and immediate support network.

Enhanced Reserve Mobilization Authorities

In the National Defense Authorization Act for Fiscal Year 2012, Congress authorized the Service Secretaries to mobilize units and individuals in support of pre-planned combatant command missions for up to 365 consecutive days. In the current defense strategy, the President and Secretary of Defense have stated that while

conventional ground forces will be reduced, Special Forces will be increased over the next five years, and a key component of the new strategy seems to be the establishment of a rotational presence in Europe, the Middle East, and anywhere US interests are threatened. Some have called this a "lily pad" approach, and it potentially dovetails with an operational view of the Reserve components.

What is your assessment of the authority to order members of the Selected Reserve to active duty for preplanned missions in support of the combatant commanders (10 USC 12304b)?

This authority aids Services by allowing for planned Reserve Component mobilizations when making decisions on restructuring and employing their forces. Utilization of the Guard and Reserve in the rotational support to COCOMs not only maintains higher readiness levels across the Total Force, but provides an operational reprieve for Active Component units to optimize full-spectrum training opportunities at home station. I consider this a critical component recovering and improving the readiness of the Total Force.

Does this authority facilitate placing members and units of the Selected Reserve in the planned rotation cycle for deployments for continuing missions?

This authority allows the use of RC forces in support of pre-planned and reoccurring Combatant Commander rotational requirements while also allowing the services to properly resource and prepare RC units for missions. This authority maintains the allotted preparation time for RC members to inform their employers or schools and make preparations for the family during their deployment.

Are the other mobilization authorities adequate to mobilize members and units of the Selected Reserve for emerging requirements where it is not feasible to include information about the deployment in budget materials for the fiscal year of the deployment?

The current set of Authorities provides the Department access under practically every conceivable condition. In regards to emergent requirements, those not planned for in the budgetary process we would utilize section 12304 of title 10, United States Code, which results from a Presidential Authorization and has been used for addressing emergent requirements (Ebola, Haiti). At this time we rely on a Declaration of National Emergency which provides access to the RC through section 12302 of such title. However, should the Declaration of National Emergency not be renewed, section 12304 would be the only authority available to address emergent requirements.

What is your assessment of the operational Reserve and how it will fit into this paradigm of smaller, more lethal forces rotating into and out of many locations of strategic interest?

The United States currently has the best equipped, trained, and experienced Reserve Component since the Second World War. To that end, the Department is looking to determine where the use of the Reserve Component might add value not only to the Nation generally, but directly to the Active Component as well. One example would be to direct some missions to the Reserve Component where training and readiness levels are more easily achievable. This would release the Active Component to train on more complex missions. If confirmed, I look forward to exploring additional capabilities and uses for the Reserve Component.

What is your understanding of the appropriate size and makeup of the reserve components in light of the defense strategy?

Each of the seven Reserve Components is unique in how it is employed and organized. I see a more robust use of the Reserve Component in the future; however, we must be prudent in understanding the opportunities of capabilities resident in the RC as we prepare our force to meet increasingly complex mission requirements.

Military Quality of Life

The Committee is concerned about the sustainment of key quality of life programs for military families, such as family support, child care, education, employment support, health care, and morale, welfare and recreation services, especially as DOD's budget declines.

If confirmed, what military qualify of life programs would you consider a priority, and how would you work with the Services, combatant commanders, family advocacy groups, and Congress to sustain them?

If confirmed, I would continue to prioritize quality of life programs that promote the well-being and resilience of Service members and their families. Providing the greatest possible access to programs such as family life counseling; spouse education and employment support; fitness opportunities; morale, welfare, and recreation; and high quality child care, supports and enhances military family readiness, and ultimately mission readiness. I am also committed to nurturing safe and strong military families through the prevention of, and coordinated community response to, domestic violence and child abuse and neglect. If confirmed, I will work with stakeholders across the Department to sustain these programs, while ensuring good stewardship of public funds and appropriate return on investment.

Family Readiness and Support

What do you consider to be the most important family readiness issues for service members and their families?

If confirmed, I will make family readiness issues one of my priorities. Family readiness systems, services and programs must work in concert to support families in balancing work and family life while meeting mission needs. If confirmed, I will support, prioritize and appropriately resource timely access to quality child care, both on and off military installations. The Secretary's Force of the Future initiative has already taken significant steps, to include extending child care center hours, to help improve family readiness. Military spouse employment continues to present a particular challenge as our Service members and their families move from location to location. If confirmed, I will work to ensure that we continue to enhance the education and employment of our military spouses.

If confirmed, how would you ensure that family readiness needs are addressed and adequately resourced?

Although we are currently in an era of declining budgets, the Department's continued emphasis on meeting family readiness needs is essential to maintaining a strong force. If confirmed, I would focus on understanding the needs of our military personnel and their families through a continuous dialogue with those who serve as well as robust research and evaluation. If confirmed, I will work with stakeholders to sustain programs that best meet these needs, while ensuring good stewardship of public funds.

If confirmed, how would you ensure support is provided to reserve component families related to mobilization, deployment and family readiness, as well as to active duty families who do not reside near a military installation?

I will promote a full range of services for Active, Reserve and National Guard members and their families. The reserve component is both integral and essential to the readiness of the Total Force and the defense of our Nation. I will endeavor to provide reserve component families with broadest access to resources while recognizing their unique needs as compared to the active component. A coordinated, community-based network of care, encompassing support and services provided by the Department of Defense and the Department of Veterans Affairs, as well as through other federal, state, local, non-profit and private providers, can be extremely effective in serving Service members and their families not residing on or near military installations. Although we are currently in an era of declining budgets, the Department's continued emphasis on meeting family readiness needs is essential to maintaining a strong force. Family support programs need to meet the needs of military families across the Total Force, wherever they live: on military installations, near military installations, or far from military installations. If confirmed, I will work with stakeholders across the Department to understand the needs of our military personnel and their families by fostering a continued dialogue with those who serve, as well as through research and assessment.

If confirmed, how would you ensure support is provided to reserve component families related to mobilization, deployment and family readiness, as well as to active duty families who do not reside near a military installation?

Please see above response.

Department of Defense Schools in CONUS

Some have questioned the continuing need for DOD-operated schools for military dependent children within the Continental United States (CONUS).

In light of the Administration's request for additional Base Realignment and Closure authorities and current fiscal constraints, should DOD establish or update its criteria for the continued operation of DOD schools within CONUS?

The Department of Defense understands the importance of education and the role it plays in the success, stability, readiness, and retention of our Service members and their families. The Department is committed to quality educational opportunities for all military children, while balancing cost and exploring all options and alternatives.

In 2013, the Department initiated a study to consider the need for DoD to own and operate DoD Schools within the United States and to evaluate other options. Informed by the RAND Institute Research Report "CONUS Education Options Assessment" the Department has initiated a comprehensive assessment. We intend this review to establish a framework for assessing options—among them, maintaining the status quo—considering location-specific issues like cost, unique stakeholder equities, local education authorities, and state law, for each of the fifteen impacted installations, including those with special arrangements.

Do you believe there continues to be a need for DOD to provide secondary education for dependents in CONUS? If so, why?

The President and the Department of Defense (DoD) view preserving and strengthening military families as critical to our national security. Military families bear an extraordinary burden for our freedom and the availability of quality education options is a critical quality of life factor. While kindergarten-grade 12 education is not a core mission of DoD, the education options available to military families remain a critically important factor of quality of life.

More than 90% of school age dependents of military members attend public schools operated by local education agencies (LEA's) in the United States. The 2008 National Defense Authorization Act DAA authorized the Secretary of Defense to utilize defense-wide operations and maintenance funds to provide resources to Local Education Agencies (LEAs) who educate military-connected students. The overarching goal of this authority is to use this competitive grant program to support the expansion of educational opportunities for children from military families attending U.S. public schools through a competitive grant program. As such, this investment has resulted in significant gains in student achievement, increased learning opportunities and educator professional development, and has enhanced transition support programs for over 500,000 military connected students in 1,500 public schools.

If confirmed, how would you approach the task of eliminating DOD-operated schools in CONUS?

If confirmed, I will consider the RAND study's findings and the Department's comprehensive assessment, in addition to seeking input from the military community, advocacy and professional groups, and state and local educational agencies, in determining the best options for providing education support for military families. I will do this in consultation with stakeholders across the Department of Defense and in collaboration with Congress.

Community Support for Military Families with Special Needs

If confirmed, how would you ensure that service members with special needs family members relocate to new duty stations where special needs services are available?

The Department's current policies require the Military Services to screen and identify military family members with medical and educational needs before the Service member-sponsor's change of duty station to ensure that those needs can be met at the prospective new location. The Department has made tremendous progress towards standardizing the screening process, including the forms involved, the data collected, and the procedures followed by the Military Services and individual installations in order to streamline and minimize—to the greatest extent possible—the stress associated with the relocation process. If confirmed, I will do my best to ensure that case management, medical, educational, and personnel assignment functions work in concert in a straightforward, and consistent fashion, to ensure that our families with special needs receive the best possible support and services before, during, and after a move.

If confirmed, how would you ensure outreach to those military families with special needs dependents so they are able to obtain the support they need?

If confirmed, I will continue to explore and utilize all available options to enhance the Department's efforts to communicate with military families with special needs dependents. Successful outreach requires that both families and engaged professionals understand where information can be sought and how services and referrals can be accessed. Like all military families, it is important to engage our military families with special needs dependents, where they live and thrive, as well as online (via websites, webinars, social media outlets, and digital strategies) and through more traditional print media. In addition, it is critical to train our leaders to identify and resolve issues affecting their Service members with special needs dependents through timely referrals to caring experts well equipped to assist in addressing concerns.

Morale, Welfare, and Recreation

If confirmed, what challenges do you foresee in sustaining MWR programs in the future fiscal environment of the Department?

The continued vitality and relevance of MWR programs depends on sound management, meeting command and customer needs, a predictable stream of non-appropriated revenue, and solid appropriated fund support of mission essential and community support programs. It is imperative that we ensure access to quality programs, information and resources regardless of where our Service members and their families are located. Changes in our basing, deployment patterns and force structure will continue to have a significant impact on our ability to deliver quality of life programs to our military families. With more than 75% of military families now living off installation, there is an increasing need for partnerships and support from local governments, school systems and businesses to ensure we continue to provide comprehensive, accessible, and affordable quality of life programs.

If confirmed, I will work to ensure that we continue to provide these important services to our Service members and their families.

Commissary and Military Exchange Systems

What is your view of the need for modernization of business policies and practices in the commissary and exchange systems? What are the most promising avenues for change to achieve modernization goals? What should the Department do to make the commissary system budget-neutral?

Commissary and exchange programs are important elements of the Service members' compensation package and contribute to the quality of life of military personnel and their families. The fiscal challenges the Department is facing demand that we evaluate all options to optimize these benefits to ensure our military families get the best value from the commissary and exchange system. I agree with public comments by the Department's Deputy Chief Management Officer (DCMO) that optimization of the commissary and exchange system should drive the budget, rather than budget-focused cuts that would reduce the commissary and exchange benefit. Strategies that give commissaries flexibilities to operate more like a commercial grocer while maintaining current savings and service levels will preserve the commissary benefit while decreasing the reliance on appropriated fund subsidies. I will work with the DCMO to explore and test several business strategies various options recommended by the Military Compensation and Retirement Modernization Commission (MCRMC) and a study by the Boston Consulting Group (BCG).

What is your view of proposals to consolidate, eliminate, or privatize commissaries and exchanges in certain areas where they are duplicative of services readily available at reasonable cost in the community?

In my view, the commissaries make important contributions to the quality of life of our Service members and their families and I would not recommend the elimination of the commissary and exchange system unless the Department can identify a more cost effective means of providing this valued benefit.

Section 651 of the National Defense Authorization Act (NDAA) for Fiscal Year (FY) 2016 requires the Department to submit to the Committees on Armed Services of the Senate (SASC) and the House of Representatives (HASC), not later than March 1, 2016, a report that addresses the privatization of the defense commissary system and the military exchange system, in whole or in part. Section 651 also requires the Comptroller General to submit a report to the SASC and HASC that assesses the above-referenced report from the Department. If confirmed, I intend to review these reports closely to help determine to assess whether such proposals should be considered.

Additionally, I have reviewed the MCRMC report and its recommendations regarding consolidation of the military resale system. Based on the BCG study's findings, it is my understanding that there are opportunities for the commissary and exchange systems to achieve operating efficiencies through enhanced collaboration and the development of common business systems and common business practices and that full consolidation is not presently required.

In your view, why has the Department been resistant to implementing a pilot program to test privatization of the Defense commissary system?

It is my understanding that as required by section 651 of the NDAA for FY16, the Department will provide a report to the SASC and HASC that examines the potential privatization of the defense commissary system. If confirmed, I look forward to reviewing the results of such report carefully in determining whether a pilot program to test privatization should be established. Nevertheless, I believe that we must be prudent in how we address proposed changes to the defense commissary system.

The suggestion that the commissary system be privatized is not new, and the Department has addressed this question many times. Since the 1920s, commissary privatization has been a topic of discussion and debate (e.g., why is the military in the grocery business). The conclusion reached by those past debates, and associated studies, is that full privatization is not an effective method of reducing the Department's budget for several reasons. Part of delivering the commissary benefit requires that the Defense Commissary Agency (DeCA) operate where Service members are located, even when it is not economically beneficial to the Department. DeCA operates in remote and overseas locations and must leverage the sales from the large stateside stores to support them. These remote and overseas locations are not attractive places to operate for commercial grocers, because they lose money. Over 40 percent of DeCA's appropriated budget provides commissary service in overseas and remote locations.

It has been suggested that the Department explore having commercial grocers take over some commissary stores, presumably the larger, profitable, stateside stores. However, if only some commissary stores were privatized, a substantial appropriated fund subsidy still would be required to service the military mission and authorized patrons in those remote and overseas areas. Additionally, if not all stores were privatized, the savings at remaining stores would decrease with DeCA's reduced buying power and increase the price of goods to commissary patrons. We must also be mindful of the domino effect the commissary has on the exchange system and morale, welfare and recreation (MWR) programs. It is well established that commissaries act as the "draw" for the military exchange system and that the loss of a commissary will result in reduced exchange earnings. This, in turn, would result in fewer exchange dollars being available to fund important MWR activities.

In short, the proposal for commissary privatization is complex and we would need to evaluate carefully the potential effect of privatization on the entire military resale ecosystem.

DOD Civilian Personnel Workforce

As the Department of Defense draws down its management headquarters functions, managers will have to make tough choice on the consolidation of functions and employees.

What is your view of a civilian employee retention system that incentivizes performance above all other factors when considering which employees to retain in a limited headquarters environment?

The Department is diligently working on a plan to establish procedures for implementing reductions of civilian positions in the Department, making the determination of which employees will be separated primarily on the basis of performance. I firmly believe that such a system will enable the Department to tailor workforce reductions in targeted ways to better align to mission and workload, minimize disruption, and retain those employees who most contribute to mission accomplishment.

If confirmed, what would be your role in the consolidation and elimination of duplicative and unnecessary positions within the Office of the Undersecretary of Defense for Personnel and Readiness?

The Office of the Under Secretary of Defense for Personnel and Readiness has already made great strides to consolidate or eliminate duplicative and unnecessary positions by reorganizing and delayering. If confirmed, I will lead the continued effort to improve the efficiency of the Personnel and Readiness enterprise.

What additional ideas do you have to more efficiently manage the Department's civilian employees?

Secretary Carter announced his goal to build the Force of the Future in order for the Department to maintain our competitive edge in bringing top talent to serve the nation in March 2015. The Secretary then directed me to examine the Department's civilian and military personnel practices, and to identify creative and modern ways to efficiently manage the force, upgrade the Department's systems and processes, and improve the Department's ability to attract the best talent. To that end, I have led an effort to design several Force of the Future initiatives in an effort to efficiently manage the Department's civilian employees.

If confirmed, I will continue to lead the effort in developing and implementing Force of the Future initiatives, and I will continue to work with all stakeholders to identify future workforce efficiencies to manage the civilian workforce.

Do you feel the new performance management system will properly address the issue of employee performance reviews and ratings?

Yes. The Department's new performance management system, the Defense Performance Management and Appraisal Program, will focus on improving overall performance management through on-going and continuous supervisor and employee involvement. The program links organizational mission and goals to individual performance plans and ensures regular feedback during the appraisal cycle between employees and supervisors, resulting in increased employee engagement, morale, and effectiveness, and affording supervisors the ability to make meaningful distinctions in their evaluations of employee performance. The Defense Performance Management and Appraisal Program will emphasize and promote timely recognition and reward of employee contributions throughout the rating cycle.

If confirmed, I will evaluate the new system to ensure that the Department fully realizes a culture that embraces and supports a high-performing workforce, emphasizes the importance of employee engagement, and acknowledges the critical role of supervisors in effective performance management.

Do managers have adequate tools to incentivize employee performance?

Performance incentives and recognition are important elements in the Department's efforts to retain talent and ensure an engaged workforce, and I believe that supervisors have sufficient tools to incentivize and recognize employee performance.

If confirmed, I will strive to ensure that supervisors across the Department will continue to use all available tools at their disposal to effectively incentivize and recognize employee performance. In addition, I would work with all stakeholders, the Administration, and Congress to identify and implement new authorities as needed.

Management Headquarters Reductions

The Department of Defense is currently under a statutory mandate to reduce headquarters staff by 25%.

If confirmed, will you commit to working with the DCMO to track the Office of the Secretary of Defense and the individual services' progress towards the 25-percent headquarters reductions?

I will commit to working in support of the DCMO-led initiative to track progress towards the 25-percent headquarters reductions.

What progress has the Office of the Secretary of Defense made thus far on the 25-percent reductions?

The DCMO, with support from the Deputy Secretary of Defense, has instituted two reviews designed to identify headquarters elements for potential reductions – redefining Major Headquarters Activities and "delayering." The Office of the Under Secretary of Defense for Personnel & Readiness (P&R) has taken an active role in each of these initiatives and to date has been able to identify, in broad terms, offices within all of P&R that will be assigned portions of the 25-percent cuts.

Do you agree that the Department of Defense should strive to eliminate duplicative functions?

I agree that the Department should strive to eliminate duplicative functions. During the P&R delayering initiative I specifically asked the Services for their recommendations and input on anything that P&R is currently performing that they would consider duplicative.

Do you believe that the process for deciding which functions are to be eliminated should be streamlined through each service?

I believe much can be achieved by OSD and the Services coming together to identify functions that can be eliminated or streamlined.

Acquisition Workforce

The Department of Defense acquisition workforce has been the subject of a large quantity of reports and legislation.

What is your view on giving more acquisition authority to the Service Chiefs?

In view of the recent statutory changes giving more acquisition authority to the Service Chiefs, if confirmed, I will continue to work with the Under Secretary of Defense for Acquisition, Technology and Logistics, Frank Kendall, and the Services, to ensure any associated manpower, personnel, and training requirements are appropriately addressed.

In what ways can we better train military personnel to be acquisition professionals?

I believe that we must constantly seek to improve on and provide opportunities for the training, education, and development of our acquisition professionals. If confirmed, I will continue to support the Under Secretary of Defense for Acquisition, Technology, and Logistics, Frank Kendall, in ensuring the continued development of military personnel as acquisition professionals.

How do you envision an acquisition workforce that holds the leadership accountable for cost overruns on procurement contracts?

Although I believe it would be more appropriate if those responsible for procurement policies and practices addressed the issue of accountability for cost overruns, I believe that having and maintaining a properly trained workforce is a key element of minimizing the risk or potential for cost overruns. Accordingly, if confirmed, I will continue to support the Under Secretary of Defense for Acquisition, Technology, and Logistics, Frank Kendall, in his efforts with respect to ensuring acquisition workforce personnel policies and training requirements are appropriately addressed.

Do you see an advantage to having a professional military acquisition workforce?

Yes, I believe that having a professional military acquisition workforce, balanced with a government civilian acquisition workforce, is advantageous. If confirmed, I will continue to support the Under Secretary of Defense for Acquisition, Technology, and Logistics, Frank Kendall, in his efforts with respect to recapitalizing, developing, and sustaining the professional acquisition workforce.

GI Bill Benefits

Congress passed the Post-9/11 Veterans Educational Assistance Act in 2008 ("Post-9/11 GI Bill) that provides generous educational benefits for service members who have served at least 90 days on active duty since 9/11.

What is your assessment of the impact of the Post-9/11 GI Bill on recruiting and retention, including the provision of transferability for continued service?

Given that the Post-9/11 GI Bill has been active only since 2009, its full impact on recruitment and retention is only starting to emerge, but by all accounts it is a valued benefit. The Department has sponsored a study with RAND National Defense Research Institute to review education benefits for Service members, including the benefits of the Post-9/11 GI Bill, and their impacts on recruiting and retention. We expect to see the study results later this summer.

Would you recommend that the Department use transferability more sparingly as a retention incentive?

Transferability encourages our career Service members to stay in uniform and share the benefits they earned with their family members, while it remains a benefit Service members appear to value highly. The Department has sponsored a study with RAND National Defense Research Institute to review education benefits for Service members, including the benefits of the Post-9/11 GI Bill, and their impacts on recruiting and retention. Until the RAND study is complete in the summer of 2016, it would be premature to support adjustments to the Post-9/11 GI Bill benefits or changes in eligibility requirements for those benefits.

If confirmed, I will continue to assess the need for legislative modifications to the Post-9/11 GI Bill.

Personnel Policy Implementation

What is your understanding of your responsibility, if confirmed, to inform and consult with this Committee and other appropriate Committees of Congress on the implementation of policies directed by law?

If confirmed, I will comply with all requirements to inform and consult with the appropriate Congressional Committees of jurisdiction on the implementation of personnel, manpower and readiness policies as directed by law.

What is your understanding of the Department's obligation and authority to implement personnel policies to improve efficiency within the Department?

It is my understanding that the Department, under the direction of the Secretary, has both the authority and obligation to evaluate and implement the most effective personnel policies while improving efficiency within the Department. These policies must not compromise operational readiness or the well-being of our Service members, their families and civilian personnel.

What is your understanding on the timeframe in which personnel policies directed by law must be implemented by the Department?

The personnel policies directed by law must be implemented in the timeliest method within the given resources and while ensuring the most effective and efficient outcome for the Total Force.

Congressional Oversight

In order to exercise its legislative and oversight responsibilities, it is important that this Committee and other appropriate committees of the Congress are able to receive testimony, briefings, and other communications of information.

Do you agree, if confirmed for this high position, to appear before this Committee and other appropriate committees of the Congress?

Yes.

Do you agree, if confirmed, to appear before this Committee, or designated members of this Committee, and provide information, subject to appropriate and necessary security protection, with respect to your responsibilities as the Under Secretary of Defense for Personnel and Readiness?

Yes.

Do you agree to ensure that testimony, briefings, and other communications of information are provided to this Committee and its staff and other appropriate Committees?

Yes.

Do you agree to provide documents, including copies of electronic forms of communication, in a timely manner when requested by a duly constituted Committee, or to consult with the Committee regarding the basis for any good faith delay or denial in providing such documents?

Yes.

www.ingramcontent.com/pod-product-compliance
Lightning Source LLC
Chambersburg PA
CBHW081426280526
45788CB00009B/3236